Messages FROM YOUR **TEACHER**

Teacher Created Materials, Inc.
6421 Industry Way
Westminster, CA 92683
www.teachercreated.com

©2003 Teacher Created Materials, Inc.

Made in U.S.A.

ISBN 0-7439-3203-X

Managing Editor: Karen Goldfluss, M.S. Ed.

Editor: Gisela Lee, M.A.

Art Director: CJae Froshay

Cover Design: Barb Lorseyedi

Line Art: Teacher Created Materials

Imaging: Ralph Olmedo, Jr., Rosa C. See

All Artwork ©Mary Engelbreit Inc.

www.maryengelbreit.com

Table of Contents

Introduction

Messages from Your Teacher is a useful book for any teacher who wants to send special and important messages, reminders, and notes home to parents or give awards and recognition to students for their efforts. This book is broken up into four sections.

❑ **Parent Notes and Reminders**—There are many times throughout the year when a teacher will need to send a written letter or note to parents concerning their children. However, sometimes it is difficult to find the exact words you want when you need them. Often, some teachers may simply not have enough time to compose the appropriate letter or note. This section provides teachers with a variety of form letters and written communications that they can send to their students' parents. Some of these letters can be directly copied and any missing information may be filled out on the copies. Others are letters or notes that teachers can write or type on personal or school stationery.

❑ **Invitations and Student Reminders**—This section of the book provides the teacher with parent and student invitations to various types of school events, such as back-to-school night, open house, book fairs, class performances, etc. There are also notes and reminders specifically tailored to students. Some of these directly remind students when they are missing assignments or when they are due, when students need to complete assigned readings, etc. This section provides teachers with written communications that they can give directly to students and parents.

❑ **Awards and Certificates**—It is always important to positively reinforce the efforts of students. With this philosophy in mind, this section of the book offers a wide assortment of awards and certificates which acknowledge the accomplishments of students (and sometimes parents, too) in different areas. Some awards recognize student efforts in completion of homework assignments, being classroom helpers, special accomplishments, creativity, etc. Some certificates recognize the student efforts in spelling, creativity, reading and other subject areas, and grade-level graduation or advancement. These special awards and certificates offer students praise and recognition for their hard work and effort in various subject areas and social situations.

❑ **Decoratives and Calendar Templates**—This section offers teachers a collection of clip art, decorative stationery, and reusable monthly calendars. The clip art can be used to decorate bulletin boards and student projects. The decorative stationery can be used for any special notes or reminders that teachers may want to send home to parents or other teachers. The reusable monthly calendars provide teachers with blank templates that can be copied and used every school year. They can be used to write special plans, weekly/monthly meetings and appointments, and other useful information throughout the school year. Teachers can personalize and then reproduce copies of the calendar so that each student receives a copy to use throughout the year. Include special events, positive sayings, and friendly reminders on each calendar month. Then, make copies and assemble the months into a calendar for each student. You may wish to three-hole punch the pages and have students keep the calendars in a section of their notebooks. Students can add their own information and notes as well.

Introductory Letter to Parents

Dear Parents,

I am pleased to take this opportunity to introduce myself to you and to welcome your child to my class. A good learning experience is built on a cooperative effort among parent, child, and teacher. I look forward to the work and growth we will all accomplish this year.

My expectations for conduct and academic standards are high. With your participation both in and out of the classroom, we can look forward to a productive, creative, and enjoyable year together. In the past, I have had many parents volunteer their time in the classroom, and I encourage this because it provides opportunities for more children to receive personal attention. If you are interested in volunteering, please let me know. This can be done on a weekly, bi-weekly, or occasional basis. Any help you can give will be warmly appreciated.

You can also help by providing me with any information that will aid me in better understanding your child. Some things I am interested in include the following:

- Important experiences that may be affecting your child's state of mind (death in the family, a best friend moving away, loss of a pet, etc.)
- Special medical needs
- Study habits at home
- Television viewing habits
- After-school activities and special interests
- Feelings toward school
- Conflicts among family members

Although I am interested in anything that could be affecting your child, it is not necessary for you to reveal personal information. Please know that anything you do say will be kept in the strictest confidence.

Again, welcome! Please feel free to contact me about any questions or concerns you may have. My classroom door is always open, and messages can be left for me with our school secretary, to which I will respond as soon as possible.

Sincerely,

_____

Request for Information

Dear Parents,

To help me know more about your child, I would appreciate your help in completing the sentences below and a short descriptive paragraph about your child on the back of this paper. Please return this form to me by _____.

Thank you for assisting me in getting acquainted with your child.

Sincerely,

_____

Child's Name: _____

Parents' Names: _____

Date: _____

My child likes to be called _____.

My child likes to _____

_____

_____.

The thing my child enjoys about school is_____

_____

_____

My child participates after school in _____

_____

_____.

One thing I really enjoy about my child is_____

_____.

Classroom Rules

Dear Parents,

We are off to a good start for the school year. The children are enthusiastic and eager to tackle their new curriculum.

To help ensure a successful school experience, we have developed the following classroom rules:

Please review our class rules with your child to be sure he or she understands them fully. Both you and your child should sign the tear-off section below and return it to class tomorrow.

Thank you for your support.

Sincerely,

_____

- -

I have reviewed the classroom rules with my child.

_____

parent signature

I understand the rules and will try to follow them this school year.

_____

student signature

Classroom Management

Dear Parents,

Our system of classroom behavior management is simple. I would like to explain it to you here so that when you come into the classroom, you will easily be able to read and understand our color chart.

On a classroom chart, each student has a pocket in which five color cards are kept. This chart will make students aware of their behavior and help them to self-monitor. The colors and what they represent:

♦ **Green:** super citizen!

♦ **Yellow:** warning, improper behavior

♦ **Orange:** lose one recess; time-out to think about actions

♦ **Purple:** consequence of infraction to be decided by teacher (losing recess, trash detail, loss of a privilege, etc.)

♦ **Red:** parental contact to remedy situation

I keep a record chart showing each student's color at the end of the day. At the end of the week, any student showing only yellows or greens will be rewarded. If the entire class has only yellows or greens for 10 consecutive days, we will celebrate with a class party or video.

With this system, I reinforce positive behavior. If any student persists in negative behavior, his or her parent will be contacted. Please reinforce at home that each child is responsible for his or her own behavior. Self-discipline is one of the best lessons a child can learn!

Sincerely,

_____

Class Schedule

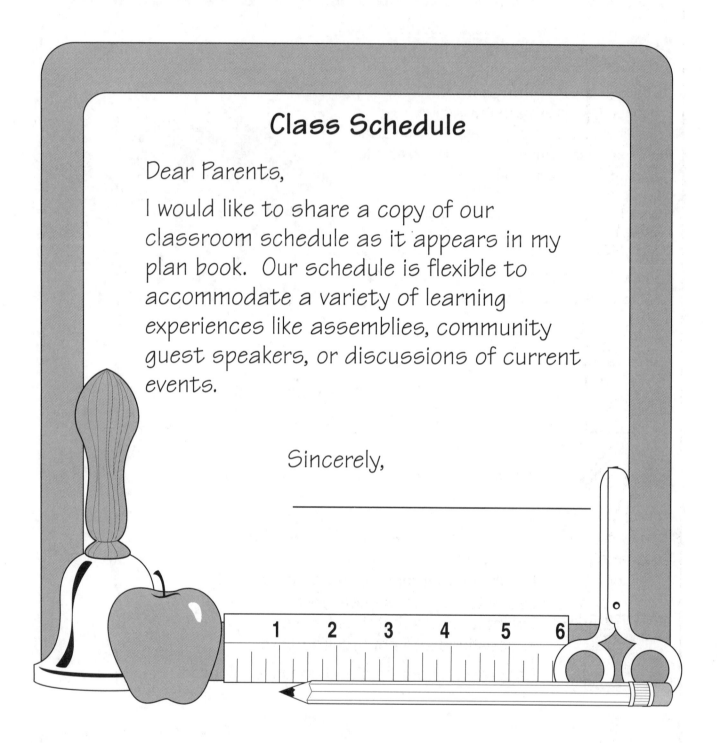

Class Schedule

Dear Parents,

I would like to share a copy of our classroom schedule as it appears in my plan book. Our schedule is flexible to accommodate a variety of learning experiences like assemblies, community guest speakers, or discussions of current events.

Sincerely,

_____

8

Student Supply List

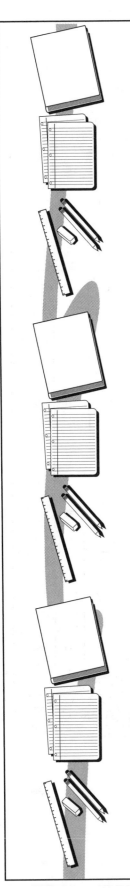

Dear Parents,

Each year I am asked, "What should my child bring to school?" This year I made a list of those items that would be especially useful throughout the school year. These include the following:

I realize that it may not be possible in all cases to send those items with your child. I want to stress that these are only suggestions and not requirements.

I appreciate your help and continued support. Please contact me if you have any questions.

Sincerely,

_____

Homework Policy

Dear Parents,

Homework has a definite place in the educational process. It is an extension of the learning experience children have during the instructional day. Homework is designed to aid the students in achieving classroom and school goals, and it should never be used to punish or merely to keep students busy.

Students in my class will be assigned approximately _____ minutes of homework per day.

The homework I give falls into one of these four categories:

1. **Remedial Drill:** This is an extension of work that has been introduced in class. This homework is an individualized drill activity designed to help strengthen the child's weak areas.

2. **Research:** This is work which involves the use of reference materials. It is often given on an extended-time basis.

3. **Unfinished Work:** This is work that is not completed in class and is within the student's capability to finish at home.

4. **Review:** This is time spent at home studying and preparing for tests.

If your child is ill but able to do schoolwork at home, I will be happy to prepare assignments that can be done without direct teacher instruction. Please call the school by the start of the school day to make arrangements for work to be picked up that afternoon.

Sincerely,

_____

Ways to Help at Home

Dear Parents,

I am often asked by parents how they can help to support their children's education at home. Here are some suggestions that may be of help to you.

❏ When booklets and papers are brought home, look at them, comment on them, and review them with your child. Show genuine interest in the work. This communicates the idea that education is important, and it encourages your child to do well in school.

❏ Talk with your child daily about school, everyday happenings, and current events.

❏ See that your child gets plenty of sleep. Encourage exercise and good nutrition.

❏ Monitor television programs. Television can be instructional and also relaxing in proper doses and at the proper times. Talk with your child about the programs he or she watches. Turn off the television during meals to facilitate conversation.

❏ Instruct your child to complete homework as early in the afternoon or evening as possible.

❏ Provide a quiet, well-lit area in which your child can study. Set up a desk or table designated for study but not far from the rest of the family. Remember to provide materials such as pens, pencils, a pencil sharpener, paper, a dictionary, crayons, glue, and scissors.

❏ Insist that homework be done away from the television and other distractions. Please be aware that some individuals work best with background music, but for others it is far too distracting. Get to know what works best for your child.

❏ Take an active interest in your child's schoolwork. Assist your child when he or she has an upcoming test and needs to study, even if that assistance is simply providing plenty of quiet time. It is also helpful to quiz your child orally on the information he or she is studying.

❏ If your child has trouble understanding something, try to help.

❏ Be aware of study strategies such as flash cards that can be shared with your child.

❏ Provide learning experiences outside of school. Parks, museums, libraries, zoos, historical sites, and family games offer good learning experiences.

❏ Encourage your child to write.

❏ Read with your child and around your child. Encourage your child to read for pleasure. Discuss what your child read, what you read together, and, where appropriate, what you are reading.

I hope this information proves helpful to you. As always, I appreciate your support.

Cordially,

_____

Homework Packet

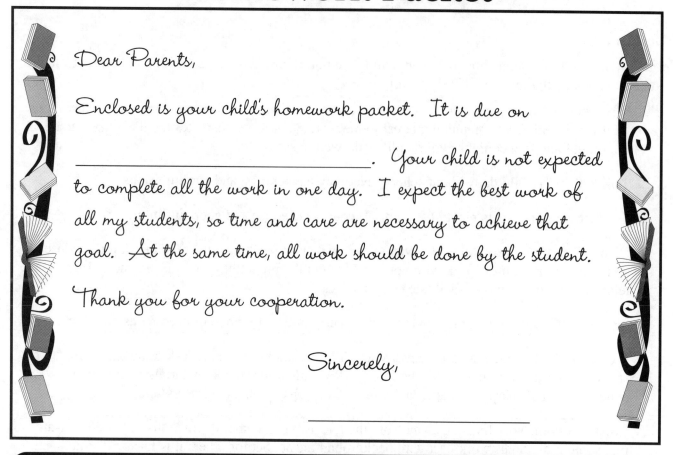

Dear Parents,

Enclosed is your child's homework packet. It is due on

_____. Your child is not expected
to complete all the work in one day. I expect the best work of
all my students, so time and care are necessary to achieve that
goal. At the same time, all work should be done by the student.

Thank you for your cooperation.

Sincerely,

_____

Date_____

Dear Parents,

Please help your child complete and correct the attached work and return
it to school on _____. The time you spend will
help your child get the most out of the assignment. Thank you for your
cooperation.

Sincerely,

_____

Helpful Reading Suggestions

Dear Parents,

Please offer suggestions on how to help your child become a better reader. Any helpful ideas would be much appreciated.

Thank you, _____
teacher

My child likes to read these types of books and wants to learn more about these topics:

_____

_____

_____

_____

_____

_____

_____

_____

_____

_____

I would like to suggest these ideas for the classroom to create more interest in reading:

_____

_____

_____

_____

_____

_____

_____

_____

_____

Volunteers

Attention!

Volunteer Help Needed

Dear Parents,

Children need to have good role models and warm, loving adults around to work with them. If you have a little extra time and the desire, your help will be greatly appreciated.

Please mark the things below that you will be willing to do at school.

❏ Read with students.

❏ Check student work.

❏ Work on cooking projects.

❏ Teach physical education games.

❏ Help with centers.

❏ Prepare teaching materials (photocopy, cut, ditto, etc.).

❏ Help limited-English speaking students.

❏ Work in a computer lab.

❏ Help with art projects.

❏ Help with science projects.

❏ Help with music or dance.

❏ Help with theatrical productions.

❏ Other (Please specify.) _____

I can use the help of volunteers during the days and times listed below. Circle those that work best for you. I will notify you of any requirements for working in the classroom and when we will need to begin. (**Note:** If you would like to help but do not have the time during the school day, materials can be sent home with your child for you to prepare in the evening and send back to school the next day. Make a note on this form if you can be a home volunteer.)

Thank you in advance for your help.

Mondays	**Tuesdays**	**Wednesdays**	**Thursdays**	**Fridays**
Time	*Time*	*Time*	*Time*	*Time*

Sincerely,

_____

_____
Volunteer's Name

_____
Child's Name

Guest Speakers

It is your child's turn to find an interesting and appropriate guest speaker to bring to class. The scheduled day and time is _____ at _____. (The time is flexible, if necessary.)

Your child must do the following:

1. Contact the speaker by letter or telephone.

2. Introduce the guest to the class.

3. Write the speaker a letter of thanks.

This page must be turned in the week before the speaker is scheduled.

Speaker:_____

Occupation:_____

Address: _____

Phone Number: _____

Why did you select this speaker? _____

_____

_____

Write your introduction for this speaker on the lines below._____

_____

_____

_____

_____

Calling on All Classroom Storytellers!

Dear Parents,

Would you like to volunteer to tell or read stories to our class? Then our classroom needs you!

At home or in the classroom, storytelling is a great way to make reading fun and entertaining for children of all ages.

Please consider becoming a classroom storyteller in your child's classroom during story hour. Fill out the form below and return it to school with your child by

_____.

_____

                  teacher   *date*

Parent's Name:_____ Child's Name:_____

❏ Yes, I would like to visit my child's class as a guest storyteller.

❏ No, I will not be able to be volunteer as a classroom storyteller at this time.

I want to ___ tell stories ___ read stories from children's books aloud ___ do both.

Suggestions for topics and/or books that you would like to tell or read stories about:

_____

_____

_____

I am available on the following days and times:

_____

_____

_____

Parental Assistance in the Classroom

WANTED!
HELPING HANDS

Date: _____

Time: _____

Activity: _____

Please return the bottom section with your signature if you can help with this activity.

Thank you for your assistance.

_____
Teacher

- -

Yes, I would be happy to help with your upcoming activity.

Name: _____

Child's name: _____

Daytime phone number: _____

Independent Study

To the parent(s) or guardian(s) of _____,

I understand your child will be absent from school on the dates of _____ through _____. I feel confident that during this time you will want to provide meaningful tasks for your child to ensure continued learning success. Please have your child complete the following items:

❏ daily journal entries

❏ attached math pages

❏ reading in _____,
   pages _____ to _____

❏ mini report on the area or event you visited during your vacation

❏ map of your travel route

❏ reading of the daily newspaper and a discussion with you of current events

❏ other: _____

_____

Your child may choose additional tasks if he or she wishes and turn them in upon your return. I look forward to seeing all of you back home safe and sound and to hearing about your many adventures.

Sincerely,

_____

Explanatory Note for Progress Reports

Dear Parents,

As progress reports go home today, I would like to send you a few words of explanation. Our progress report was designed to give you an indication of your child's growing skills and maturity. I am always concerned when putting progress reports in writing that parents or children will try to determine the child's academic future. This report is meant merely as part of the ongoing communication between school and home in terms of the current progress. Many factors go into determining future potentials.

I also caution you against making comparisons of your child's report with those of your other children or your child's classmates. I have seen many children and parents hurt and discouraged when comparing, forgetting that the progress of one child can in no way compare to the progress of another. Everyone is an individual and evaluated as such.

If you wish to discuss this report and to gain additional feedback, please feel free to contact me to arrange a conference. I will be happy to discuss any of your questions or concerns.

As always, it is a pleasure to share in the education of your child.

Sincerely,

_____

Progress Report

Student: _____ **Teacher:** _____

Room: _____ **Date:** _____

This progress report tells you about your child's academic and social growth and development over the past _____ weeks. After reading this report, please fill in the form below. Return the bottom portion by _____.

Areas of growth: _____

_____

_____

_____

Areas to work on: _____

_____

_____

_____

Suggestions: _____

_____

_____

_____

_____

_____
teacher

- -

Parent: _____ **Child:** _____

Comments: _____

_____

_____

I would like to arrange a conference time. Please contact me at _____.
phone number

Scheduling a Phone Conference

Dear Parents,

I would like to schedule a phone conference with you to discuss...

_____

_____

This will give us a great opportunity to discuss how your child is doing and take a look at any areas that may need improvement.

I would like to discuss the following topics:

❑ school work habits _____

❑ study habits at home _____

❑ overall attitude _____

❑ classroom behavior _____

❑ specific subject areas _____

❑ student interactions _____

❑ self-esteem _____

❑ other _____

Comments

_____

_____

_____

_____

_____

Thank you for your cooperation. Please complete the attached note and return it by _____.

Sincerely,

_____

Scheduling a Phone Conference *(cont.)*

Parent's Name:_____ Child's Name:_____

The best time to reach me for a phone conference is _____

This is the phone number that you can call during this time _____

Comments or topics of concern that I would like to discuss about my child are . . .

_____

_____

_____

_____

_____

_____

_____

_____

_____

_____

_____

_____

- -

Confirmation of Phone Conversation

I will call you on _____
                            day

_____ at _____ A.M./P.M.
date   *time*

_____
teacher

Pre-Conference Letters

Dear Parents,

Since the start of the school year, I have been getting to know your child, his or her interests, and how he or she learns. However, there is, of course, a great deal of time outside of school that I do not spend with your child, and certainly your perspective and experience with your child will vary to some degree from mine. In that light, I would appreciate reading your written perspective before we get together for our upcoming conference. Please take a few minutes to respond to the following questions and return them to me by _____.

Thank you for your assistance.

Sincerely,

_____

- -

Child's Name:_____   Date:_____

Parent's Name:_____

- What are your child's feelings about school, both positive and negative?

  _____

  _____

- What do you see as your child's greatest personal assets?

  _____

  _____

- In what scholastic or other areas do you think your child needs to improve?

  _____

- Who are your child's current role models and heroes?

  _____

- What would you like to see happen for your child educationally over the next school term?

  _____

  _____

Pre-Conference Letters *(cont.)*

Dear Parents,

Student's Name_____

Our conference is scheduled for _____, _____
                                          day   date

at _____ in _____. At that time, we will
           time   place

discuss _____'s work habits, test results, homework, academic
              student's name

progress, social skills, and special talents.

Please come prepared with any questions of your own. You may list them on the

response sheet below, if you wish. Please return the bottom section of this form

to me by _____.

I am looking forward to meeting with you.

                                                        Sincerely,

                                                        _____
                                                                      teacher

- -

Parent's Name:_____

Student's Name:_____

Teacher:_____

Scheduled Conference Date and Time:

☐ Yes, I will be able to meet at our scheduled time.

☐ No, I am unable to meet at the scheduled time. Please contact me at

_____ to arrange a different day and/or time.
      phone number

Some things I would like to discuss at our conference include: _____

_____

_____

                                                        _____
                                                                  parent signature

Conference Reminder and Cancellations

Dear _____,

Just to remind you, our conference is scheduled for _____
                                                                                                time

on _____. I look forward to meeting with you.
              date

Sincerely,

_____

Dear _____,

Unfortunately, I must reschedule our upcoming conference due to unavoidable circumstances. I apologize for any inconvenience this causes you. I will call you to arrange a new conference time.

Thank you for understanding.

Sincerely,

_____

Dear _____,

I am sorry we missed seeing each other for our scheduled conference time. I am sure you were unavoidably detained. Perhaps you can let me know another day and time that will suit your schedule. I am sure you are as anxious to meet and discuss your child's progress as I am.

Sincerely,

_____

Supply Requests

Dear Parents,

We are beginning a new unit of study. As always, we will be doing a variety of activities around our theme. In order to make our experience a success, we are asking for the donation of special supplies that we will need during our course of study. If you have and would like to donate any of the following, please send them to school with your child by _____.

_____

_____

_____

_____

_____

_____

_____

_____

Thank you for your assistance.

Sincerely,

_____

Supply Requests *(cont.)*

Dear Parents,

Our class will be making lots of fun projects this month. Many of our activities will require items that you may already have at home. Please take a minute to see if you have any of the following items on hand. If so, please send them with your child on or before _____.

Thank you.

_____
Teacher

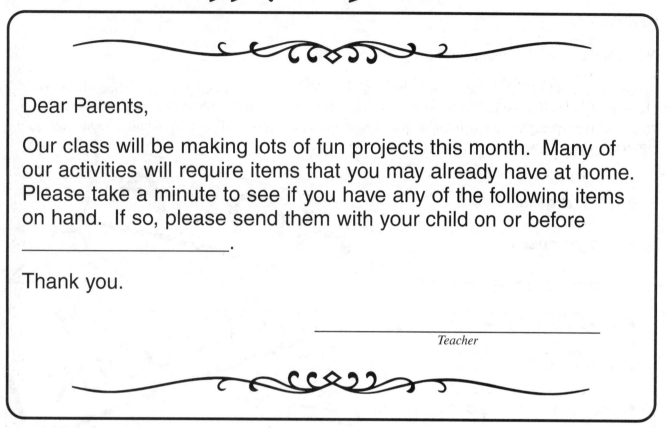

Dear Parents,

Can you help us with our _____ party? If so, please send _____ on or before _____.

Thank you.

_____
Teacher

Teach and Tell

Dear Parents,

Your child's scheduled Teach and Tell will take place on _____.

Since preschool or kindergarten, your child has probably been participating in share time. Now he or she is ready for what we call Teach and Tell. This differs from simple sharing in that the child is responsible for teaching his or her classmates a simple activity or skill. Ideas include but are not limited to the following:

- a mind game

- a logic puzzle

- a craft such as origami

- words in a foreign language

- a "how to"

- the rules of a sport or game

- an anagram

- a science experiment

- a science fact

- a math fact

- explanation of how something works

The best place to begin when choosing a topic for Teach and Tell is with your child's particular interests and hobbies. Once the decision has been made, please help your child to prepare by watching him or her rehearse, offering praise, and suggesting improvements.

Thank you for taking the time to help your child prepare for Teach and Tell. The more rehearsal he or she has, the better the presentation is likely to be.

Sincerely,

_____

Newsletters

Newsletters are invaluable tools of communication between the classroom and home. A weekly newsletter is an excellent way to keep parents/guardians apprised of different units of study, special days, and future needs. Remember, too, to let parents know about future field trips, guest speakers, holiday news, birthdays, and so forth. If possible, it is a good idea to include anecdotal materials and samples of student work.

What's News?

by Room _____

Date:

Newsletters *(cont.)*

The Class News

Week of_____

Feature of the Week

_____

_____

_____

_____

_____

_____

_____

_____

Monday	**Tuesday**	**Wednesday**	**Thursday**	**Friday**

Field Trip

We're Going on a Field Trip!

Where: _____

When: _____

Why: _____

_____

How: _____

Please bring _____

_____

Please sign the permission slip below and have your child return it by _____. Your child will not be allowed to participate without the signed permission slip.

Thank you.

_____
Teacher

My child, _____, has my permission to participate in a field trip to _____.

I understand that transportation to and from the field trip will be

❏ by school bus   ❏ by car

❏ on foot   ❏ other_____

_____   _____
date   *Parent signature*

❏ I will be happy to chaperone. Please contact me at_____.

daytime phone number

Field Trip Inquiry

Write this letter on school stationery. Otherwise, follow the format on this page.

Date

School Address

Addressee

Dear_____,

I am a teacher at_____ in

the_____District.

My_____class is learning

about_____.

A field trip to_____would be a great

experience to enhance their learning.

Please send me information concerning the cost, what a tour of the facility would include, how much time the tour would take, and the dates and times available.

Please send any additional brochures or application forms.

Thank you.

Sincerely,

_____

Teacher Note: *Always send information about the field trip site to chaperoning parents ahead of time along with information about what is expected of them as a chaperone. This will help your field trip experience to run smoothly.*

Parental Assistance for Field Trips

Dear Parents,

We need parent volunteers to accompany us as chaperones on our field trip to

_____ on

_____. We will leave school at

_____ and return at _____.

If you would like to help, please sign and return the section below.

Thank you for your assistance.

_____

Teacher

- -

Yes, I would like to attend as a chaperone on your upcoming field trip.

Name: _____

Child's name: _____

Daytime phone number:_____

SCHOOL BUS

Spelling Philosophy

Dear Parents,

Until now your child has often used "invented" spelling in much of his or her writing. Invented spelling is the formation of the written word according to the way it sounds to the child. It is a typical and natural way for emerging writers to begin shaping words. However, your child is now ready to begin looking carefully at the correct spelling of the words he or she uses.

With that in mind, we are beginning to study a set of spelling words each week. We will use the words during our lessons throughout the week, and homework will often involve them. The words can be a part of your home life as well. The following are suggested ways in which you can support your child's learning of the correct spelling for each word.

★ Together with your child, find the words in newspapers and magazines.

★ Play word games.

★ Write the words using different media (thick pens, markers, thin pens, sand, crayons, pencils, paint, makeup, etc.)

★ Do rainbow writing. The child forms the words using one color crayon. He or she then writes on top of the word in another color. Do this repeatedly for up to four or five colors.

★ Use magnetic letters on the refrigerator to spell the words.

★ Use cereal or macaroni letters to form the words.

All these methods are effective alternatives to traditional drills. The end result is the same without the corresponding drudgery.

As always, thank you for your support.

_____
Teacher

34

Bringing Home Books

Dear Parents,

Today your child is bringing home a little book. This is just one of many your child will receive this year. The little books are miniatures of the books, poems, or charts we are using in the classroom. Let your child read the book to you. Do not worry if your child does not know all the words or if he or she has merely memorized the text. This is how reading begins. Celebrate what your child can do and the interest shown in wanting to read. Thank you for taking the time to share these little books. Your involvement is critical to your child's success.

Sincerely,

_____

Bringing Home Books *(cont.)*

Dear Parents,

I am bringing this book home to read to you. Please take time tonight to listen to me read it. Help me to remember to return it to school tomorrow.

Thank you,

_____

36

Birthday Celebrations

Dear Parents,

Birthdays are special occasions, and we enjoy celebrating them at school. Please know that you are welcome to send treats to the classroom on your child's birthday, either of the edible or material kind. However, it is not necessary to send treats, and whether or not treats are present, we will be sure to take a few moments to honor your special birthday child.

Best wishes,

_____

Messy Day

We will be

_____
activity

_____
date

On _____
date

we will be _____
activity

Dress for Mess!

Overdue Work

To the Parent or Guardian of _____,

The following assignments are overdue and must be completed by _____ in order to receive credit.

_____

_____

_____

_____

_____

_____

_____

_____

_____

_____

_____

In order to promote habits of completion and satisfaction for a job well done, please have your child complete the assignments immediately and return them to me. Attach this note signed by you with the completed work.

Thank you.

_____
Teacher

_____   _____
Parent   *date*

Change in Student Behavior

_____
date

Dear _____,

I am writing this letter out of concern for _____. I have noticed a definite change in _____'s performance in class, and I was hoping you might have some insight to share with me. I am sure if we pool our resources, we can make this a positive and productive year for _____. Please let me know a convenient day and time we can meet. My phone number at school is_____.

Sincerely,

_____

Student Progress

Name_____ Date_____

Effort	Work Habits	Behavior
____ Outstanding	____ Needs some guidance to complete assignments	____ Is a Leader
____ Very Good		____ Sets a Good Example
____ Good	____ Needs constant guidance to complete assignments	____ Is Improving
____ Needs to improve		____ Forgets Self Control
____ Works Independently	____ Easily Distracted	
	____ Distracts Others	

____ If checked here, please sign and return.

_____   _____
teacher signature   *parent signature*

Note of Condolence

Teacher's Note: *Transfer these notes to personal stationery.*

Dear_____,

I was saddened yesterday to learn of_____'s death. Please accept my condolences.

name

I want to reassure you that during this time I will keep a watchful eye on_____. I will lend any support I feel is necessary.

student's name

If I can be of any help to you,_____, please let me know.

name

Sincerely yours,

_____

Note of Condolence *(cont.)*

Dear_____,

I am terribly sorry to hear about the hardship your family is going through at the present time.

I hope the situation will be remedied soon. In the meantime, I want to reassure you that I will be supportive at school for your_____,
son/daughter

_____.
name

Sincerely,

_____

Goodbye to Kindergarten Parents

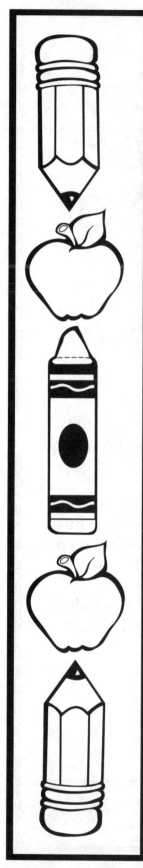
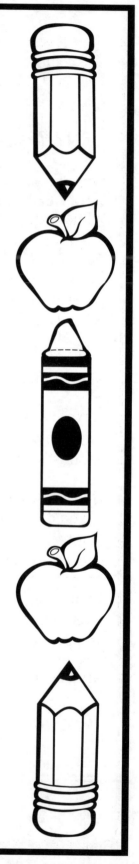

Dear Parents,

I could not let the school year draw to a close without a comment on what I think was a very special class. Happy, well-adjusted children tend to come from caring homes. Your positive attitudes toward your children's education have been reflected in their enthusiasm and willingness to learn.

I have appreciated your support in so many ways.

- Our wonderful parent volunteers have given their time and given of themselves to make our program work.

- Those of you who couldn't volunteer your time have been so generous in sending things to help us in our program. Thank you very much.

- We have had wonderful parties this year thanks to our very efficient and very well-organized room parents.

Recently, I had a talk with the class about first grade. I told them how they would be split up in different classes and have different teachers. There was a moment of silence—a flicker of dismay crossed their faces—and then came the smiles, "Oh boy! We get to eat lunch in school! We will read! We will write our own stories!" I was so proud of them. They have that magnificent self-confidence that makes them eager to reach out for the new challenge. This is what school and life are all about. They are great! They are ready! They are your children!

    Sincerely,

    _____

    44

Parent Goodbye

Dear Parents,

This has been a productive and interesting year in your child's education. I have enjoyed the part I've been able to play in contributing new ideas and experiences. Your child's eagerness and willingness to learn are a reflection of the importance you place on education.

I have appreciated your support in so many ways.

Wonderful parent volunteers gave of their time and themselves to make the program work.

Those of you who could not volunteer your time have been so supportive and generous in sending things in to help our program. A big thank you! Your behind-the-scenes support is crucial, too.

Our fun parties this year have in large part been organized by our room parents. Many others have also contributed; thanks to all of you.

Next year will be a big step for your child, appropriate for his or her capabilities. You can do much this summer to make next year an even better one. Be positive about your child's placement. Encourage your child to accept responsibility.

Help your child learn to make decisions and accept the results of those decisions. Give your child the gift of organization and a strategy to develop it. Share times that are creative, not necessarily expensive. Encourage independence, but do not expect it to be absolute. Have fun!

I am very proud of the progress that your child has made. I will enjoy watching them reach out for challenges and the future. That is what school and life are about.

My best to all of you.

Sincerely,

_____

Halloween Party

Dear Parents,

Our annual school-wide costume parade will take place on
_____ at _____. All students are invited to
come to school in costume; however, costumes are not required. Parents are
invited to attend, as well, to watch the parade and to photograph the event. The
adventurous can also come in costume!

Please remember to send your child with regular school clothes so he or she can
change out of the costume after the parade. For obvious safety reasons, please
choose costumes that are comfortable, easy to move in, and allow clear vision.
Please note that no weapons, fake blood, or gory costumes will be allowed.

Thank you

_____
Teacher

Winter Program

Dear Parents,

On _____ at _____, our school will host a winter holiday program. You and your family are invited to attend. During the program, our students will perform, and the bigger and friendlier the audience, the better.

Feel free to bring your video cameras to record the event. The winter program is always a crowd pleaser, and you will want to preserve the memories of your child's performance.

Please use the form below to let us know if you will attend our performance. We would like to have a good idea of the number who will be here so that we can plan refreshments. Return the form with your child by _____.

Thank you,

_____
Teacher

- -

Name:_____

Child's Name:_____

☐ Yes, we will be happy to attend this year's winter program. Number attending: _____

☐ No, unfortunately we will not be able to attend this year's program.

Valentine Exchange

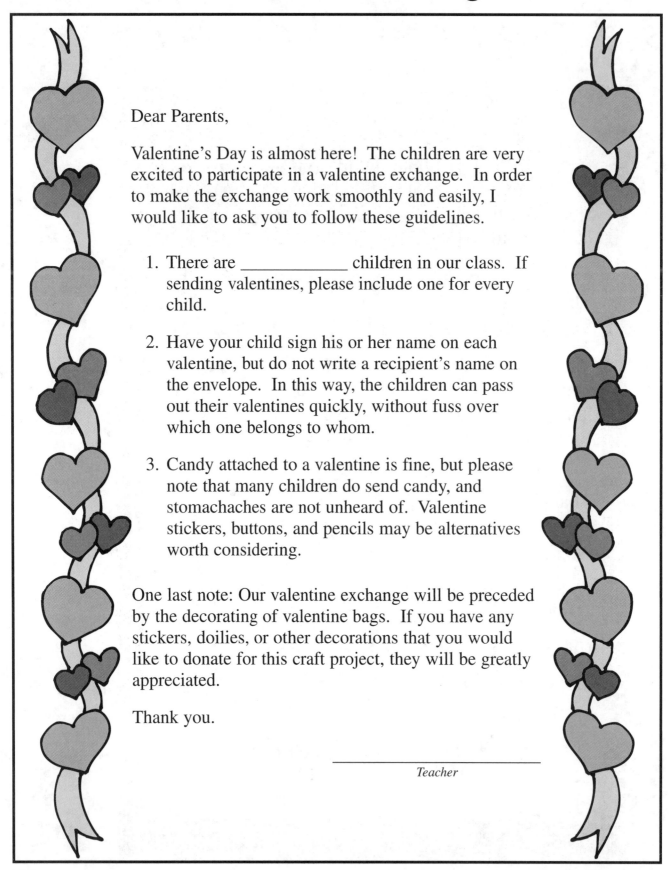

Dear Parents,

Valentine's Day is almost here! The children are very excited to participate in a valentine exchange. In order to make the exchange work smoothly and easily, I would like to ask you to follow these guidelines.

1. There are _____ children in our class. If sending valentines, please include one for every child.

2. Have your child sign his or her name on each valentine, but do not write a recipient's name on the envelope. In this way, the children can pass out their valentines quickly, without fuss over which one belongs to whom.

3. Candy attached to a valentine is fine, but please note that many children do send candy, and stomachaches are not unheard of. Valentine stickers, buttons, and pencils may be alternatives worth considering.

One last note: Our valentine exchange will be preceded by the decorating of valentine bags. If you have any stickers, doilies, or other decorations that you would like to donate for this craft project, they will be greatly appreciated.

Thank you.

_____
Teacher

Back-to-School Night Invitation

IT'S BACK-TO-SCHOOL NIGHT AND YOU ARE INVITED!

Date:

Time:

Room:

Back-to-School Night is an opportunity for parents to meet with their child's teacher and to learn more about the curriculum, activities, and events of the coming year. Your attendance is most welcome and appreciated.

See you there!

Open House Invitation

Directions: Cut along the dashed lines. Add glue along the strip as shown and place the top page (with doors) over the bottom page so that the invitation opens like a card.

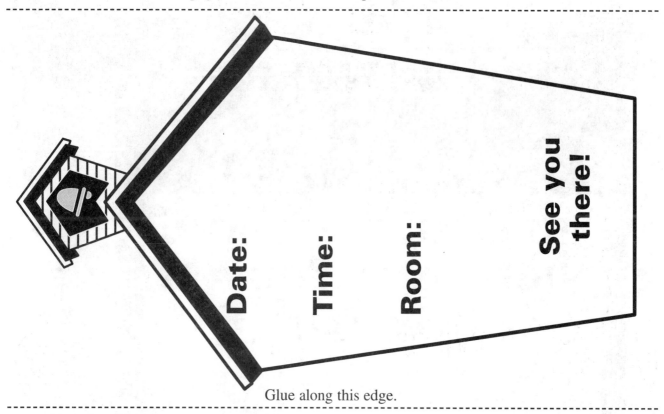

Date:

Time:

Room:

See you there!

Glue along this edge.

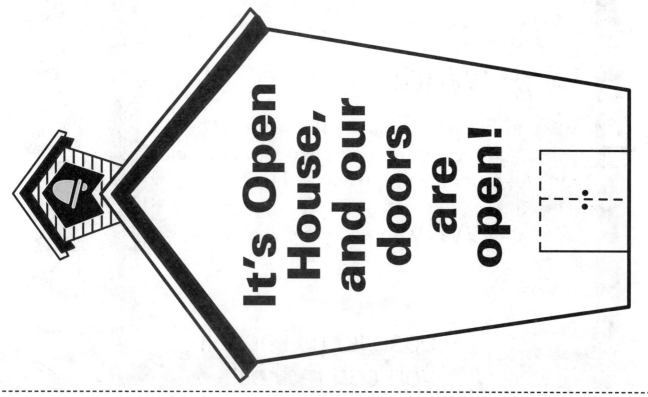

It's Open House, and our doors are open!

General Invitation

Where:

When:

Who:

Why:

Please let us know if
you can make it.

Special Invitations

You're Invited to a School Performance

Please join us as our school performs

_____. It's being performed by

_____ at _____ on _____.

Come See What's New at the School Book Fair

You are cordially invited to come to our book fair on _____ at

_____.

Behavior Contract

I will try to: _____

_____

_____

_____

for the next _____

amount of time (days or weeks)

_____

Student signature

_____

Teacher signature

_____

Date

Work Contract

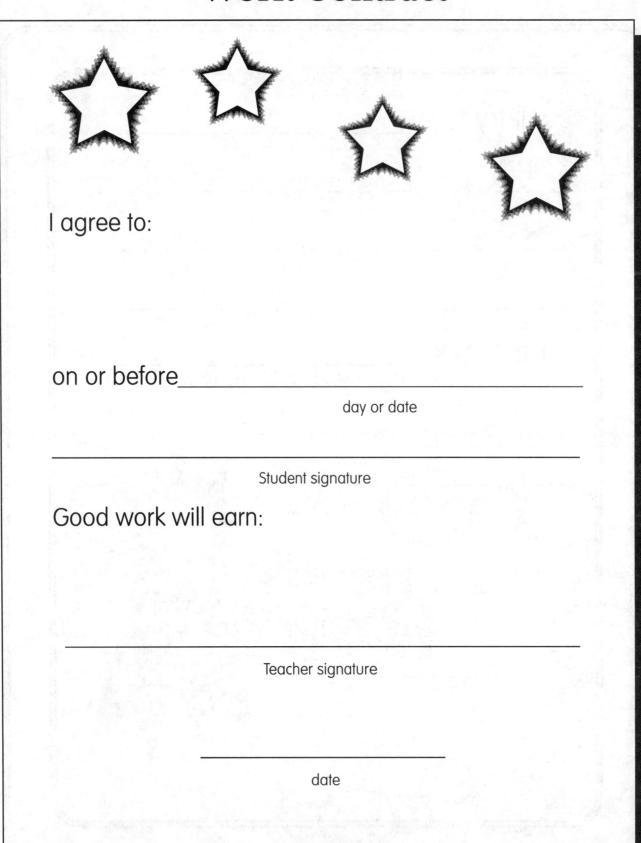

I agree to:

on or before_____
                    day or date

_____
                    Student signature

Good work will earn:

_____
                    Teacher signature

_____
                    date

Attendance Recognition

Three Cheers for

_____!

_____ had perfect attendance this week!

Congratulations!

Hip-Hip HOO-RAY!

_____

has attended school every day during this month!

Book Suggestions

You've Got to Read This!

My classmates should read!

_____

by _____

It was a great book because

_____

Check This Book Out

I loved _____

_____

It's about _____

_____

_____

_____

If you love to read, you definitely have to read this book!

Book Reading Agreements

Reading Contract

date _____

I, _____, am going to read

_____

by _____.

_____
student signature

Dive into a Book!

I plan to read

_____.

by _____ and will
complete a book
report by _____.

_____
student signature

Homework Recognition

You hit a homerun by completing all your homework this week.

Congratulations

_____!

You did an excellent job!

_____
teacher signature

Seal of Approval

_____
did a great job completing all the homework assignments!
You deserve a round of applause!
Keep up the great work!

_____
teacher signature

Student Vacation

Dear Student,

You have been working very hard and doing a good job with reading and writing in the last few weeks. I am pleased with your progress.

The time has come for a little vacation. I hope you will find some interesting things to do during that time. Be sure to tell your mom and dad that you will be available to do some work around the house!

Do not forget about reading and writing! Here are some good ideas for reading and writing activities using the newspaper:

1. Cut out words that belong to word families you have studied.
2. Collect interesting pictures. Be ready to explain what they are about.
3. Learn a new word every day. Tell what section of the newspaper it came from.
4. Collect interesting new items.
5. Read "Dear Abby" and try to think of other ways to solve the writer's problems.
6. Collect interesting cartoons and draw one of your own.
7. If your newspaper has a puzzle page for students, try to work the puzzle.
8. Look in the classified ad section. Find a job you would like to have. Try to figure out what the abbreviations in the ad stand for.
9. Design a newspaper ad for your favorite consumer item.
10. Pretend you have made an amazing discovery or invention. Write a newspaper article about yourself.

Happy vacation! Happy reading!

_____

Introductory Letter to Students (Primary)

Dear _____,
Student's name

Welcome to the _____ grade! I am glad you
are a part of our class. We will be sharing an
exciting year together, learning about _____

_____

_____

_____

I cannot wait to discover what interests you have
to share with the class.

Welcome aboard!

_____
Teacher

Grade

Introductory Letter to Students (Intermediate)

Welcome!

I am happy to welcome you to my class this year. I am looking forward to an exciting year as we share our ideas, talents, and interests.

We will make our class rules together as a class. Please begin brainstorming on the paper provided when you finish reading this letter.

This year we will be learning _____

_____

_____

_____

_____

_____

_____

_____

_____

Please feel free to tell me about any special interests or knowledge that you have. We will always be happy to explore interesting new topics as the year progresses.

If you ever have any questions or concerns, do not hesitate to bring them to my attention. All problems can be solved with openness and teamwork.

Here's to a wonderful school year!

_____
Teacher

Class Guidelines

Teacher Note: Adapt these guidelines to meet your own classroom needs. The following guides are only suggestions.

Welcome to Our Class

Our new year is under way, and I am so glad you will be a part of it.

In order to make the year run smoothly, there are some guidelines that we all need to follow. Keep these guidelines with you. They are important for you to know.

- Treat everyone with courtesy and respect.

- When the teacher or a classmate is sharing, do not interrupt.

- Do not use the teacher's or another student's supplies without asking permission.

- Listen carefully to all instructions.

- Complete all assignments neatly and on time.

Everyone is expected to know and follow these rules. If we all do so, we are sure to have a wonderful, exciting school year.

Incomplete Work

Whoops! Something is missing!

Please complete

by _____.

Just a Reminder!

Incomplete Work

The following assignment(s) is/are incomplete:

_____

_____

_____

_____

It/They must be completed by _____ in order to receive credit.

Missing Work

MISSING

_____'s Work

Room _____ reports that the following assignment is missing:

_____

_____

If found, please return it immediately to the proper authorities.

Missing Assignments

The following assignments are missing from my record book:

_____

_____

_____

If you have forgotten to turn them in, please do so now. If you have never finished them, please see me today to make a plan for completing them.

Appreciation Certificates

Thanks for the helping hand!

I couldn't have done it without you!

_____ _____
Teacher   Date

Appreciation Certificates *(cont.)*

Thank you,

_____,

from the bottom of my heart.

_____
Teacher

_____
Date

Congratulations and Appreciation

Dear _____,

Congratulations to you!

I want to tell you how pleased I am

that you _____

_____

_____.

This is a wonderful
accomplishment.
Keep it up!

Best wishes,

_____

Congratulations and Appreciation *(cont.)*

Dear

_____,

I want to thank you for the great job you have done this past year as _____.

I really appreciate you.

Sincerely,

_____

68

Thank You for Helping

Dear _____,

Thank you for helping us on our field trip

to _____. It is

people like you who make special learning

experiences possible.

Sincerely,

_____

Thank You for Helping *(cont.)*

Dear _____,

Thank you for helping in the classroom on

_____.

Without your help, we would not be able to do special projects like this.

We hope you will work with us again soon.

Sincerely,

_____

Missing Tooth

Another one for the Tooth Fairy?

Congratulations,

_____ !

from _____

(**What do you think she does with all those teeth anyway?**)

Tiiiiiimmmmm-berrrrrrr!

There goes another one!

Congratulations, _____ !

from _____

Get Well Notes

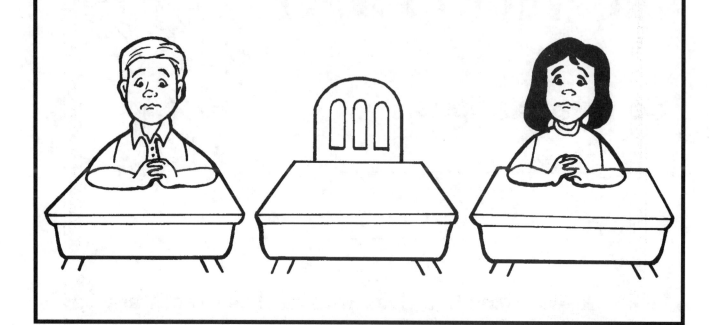

Recognition for Creativity

What a Spectacular Burst of Creativity!
Congratulations

_____ !

You did an excellent job with your project!

_____
teacher signature

Beautiful Art Award

_____

is being honored for his/her marvelous art project.

Take great pride in your creation!

_____
teacher signature

Spelling Award

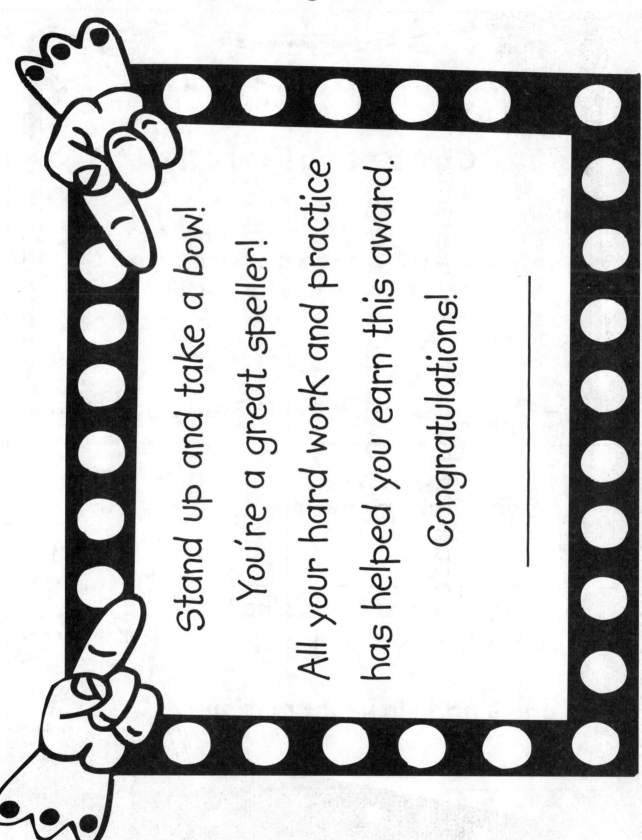

Stand up and take a bow!

You're a great speller!

All your hard work and practice

has helped you earn this award.

Congratulations!

Reading Award

Spotlight Reading Achievement

This award recognizes

_____

for completing all his/her
reading assignments.

_____
Teacher

_____
Date

Math Award

WIZARDRY

You have become a Math Wizard in

_____

Congratulations!

Science Award

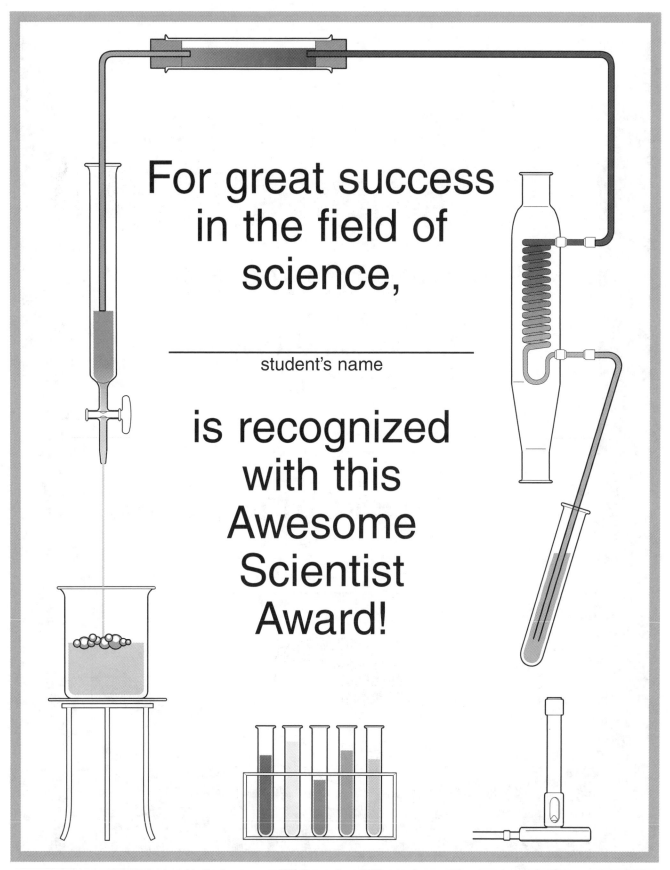

For great success
in the field of
science,

_____
student's name

is recognized
with this
Awesome
Scientist
Award!

Excellent Overall Effort

Three Cheers!

For displaying excellent overall effort in his/her classwork, today is hereby decreed

_____'s

special day!

_____   _____
date   *teacher*

Classroom Helper

Award

In recognition of being a great classroom helper, this certificate is awarded to

.

Thanks so much for all your help!

teacher

Great Teamwork Award

Great teamwork is the key to success in any classroom!

Thanks for being such a great team player!

Congratulations

_____!

_____   _____
Date   Teacher

Birthday Recognition

_____

celebrate your special day!

_____

teacher

Terrific Tickets

Teacher Note: Pass these out to students anytime you see them doing something particularly helpful or kind such as helping a classmate or showing exceptional courtesy on the playground. Offer prizes such as erasers, stickers, or free time when a student redeems five tickets.

Terrific Ticket

I caught you being terrific!

Terrific Ticket

I caught you being terrific!

Terrific Ticket

I caught you being terrific!

Terrific Ticket

I caught you being terrific!

Terrific Tickets *(cont.)*

Terrific Ticket

I caught you being terrific!

Terrific Ticket

I caught you being terrific!

Terrific Ticket

I caught you being terrific!

Terrific Ticket

I caught you being terrific!

Hooray for Me!

Teacher Note: Duplicate these awards and give them to students as they reach various milestones. One is blank to complete with your own message.

Hooray for Me! *(cont.)*

Hooray for me!

I know how to tell time.

Hooray for me!

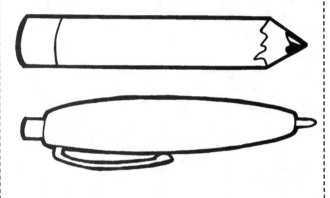

I know how to write in cursive.

Hooray for me!

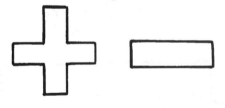

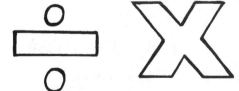

I know how to

_____ add   _____ subtract

_____ multiply   _____ divide

Hooray for me!

85

Warm Fuzzies

It is often a good idea to recognize students for their little successes each day. Use these and the following reward cards to offer a "warm fuzzy" to any student of whom you are proud.

To_____

For_____

HUG ME
I've been special today!

 **SPY**
A Good Worker!

Top Work

5-Star Day!

 # Beary Good!

Seasonal Warm Fuzzies

Vonderful!

Gobble, Gobble, Good

Super star

Sweets to the Sweet

You're a Treasure!

Somebunny Special

Certificate of Achievement

Certificate of Achievement

Terrific!

Participation

Parent

This is to certify that

_____

parent of

_____

made a difference in the life of a child.

This parent's involvement in education has made our school a better place.

With thanks and appreciation,

_____
Teacher

_____
Date

Outstanding Volunteer

Outstanding Volunteer Award

This certifies that

_____

has been an outstanding volunteer in our room during this school year!

Thank you for your special dedication!

Outstanding
Volunteer

_____
Teacher

_____
Principal

_____
Date

Goodbye Certificate

It was a

PLEASURE

having

_____

in my class this year!

_____
Teacher

_____
Date

Student Greeting

is part of our class team this year. Welcome!

Date

Teacher

Volunteer Thank You

Dear_____,

I want to take this opportunity to express my most sincere thanks for taking the time to

_____

_____.

In this day of busy schedules, it is especially gratifying to see individuals such as yourself giving freely of your time in assisting schools in meeting their educational goals for students.

I want to especially mention

_____.

Thanks for your help. Have an enjoyable and relaxing summer.

Cordially,

_____

Goodbye Letter (Primary)

Dear _____,

I have been so glad to have you in my class this year. Your smile, curiosity, and hard work made my days extra special. Thank you for being you!

Good luck next year as a _____ grader!

Yours truly,

_____

Goodbye Letter (Intermediate)

Dear _____,

This past year has been one of adventure and learning for me. I hope it has been the same for you.

I cannot tell you what a pleasure it has been to have you in my class this year. I have enjoyed watching you learn and grow from a quiet, young _____ grader to the mature, confident child you are today. Please know how proud I am of you.

I wish you all the best in your years of education to come. Always remember what you have learned here and all you have achieved. You have a right to be proud. Good luck!

Best wishes,

_____

Completed Work

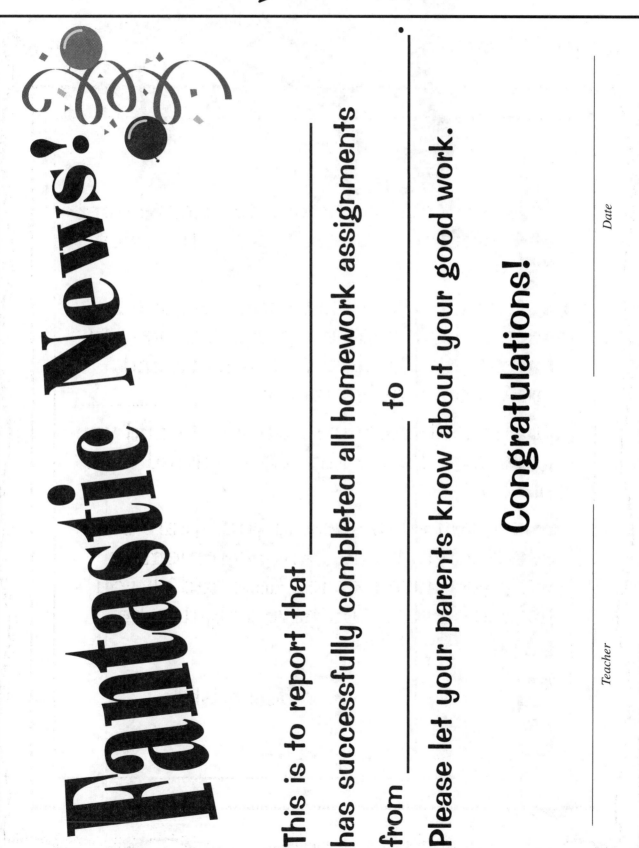

Fantastic News!

This is to report that _____

has successfully completed all homework assignments

from _____ **to** _____

Please let your parents know about your good work.

Congratulations!

_____
Teacher

_____
Date

Kindergarten Graduation

Congratulations!

You have graduated from kindergarten.

Good job!

Teacher

Principal

Date

96

Grade Advancement

Congratulations,
_____!

You are now a
_____ grader.

Good work!

Teacher

Principal

Date

Advancement Certificate

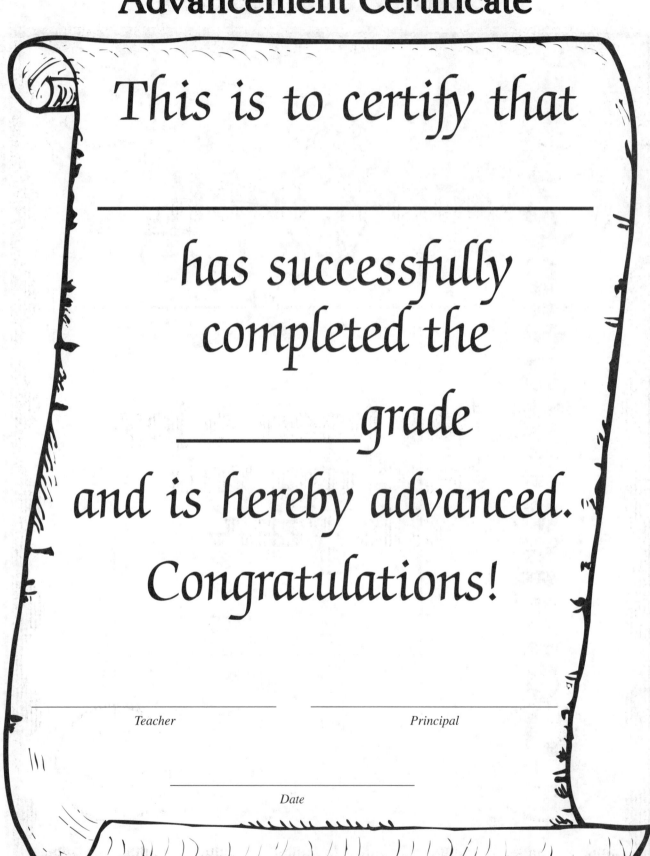

This is to certify that

_____

has successfully completed the

_____ grade

and is hereby advanced.

Congratulations!

_____   _____
Teacher   Principal

_____
Date

Farewell Certificate

Good luck,

_____

It has been a joy teaching you this year.

_____
Teacher

_____
Date

General Information

A Flyer for Parents!

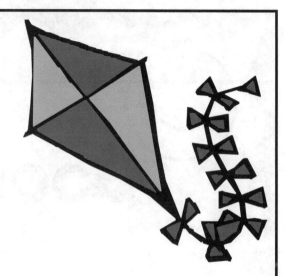

Stay Tuned!

Nameplates

Teacher Note: *Affix these nameplates to each student's desk or table at the start of the new year to help you and the students get to know one another.*

Nameplates *(cont.)*

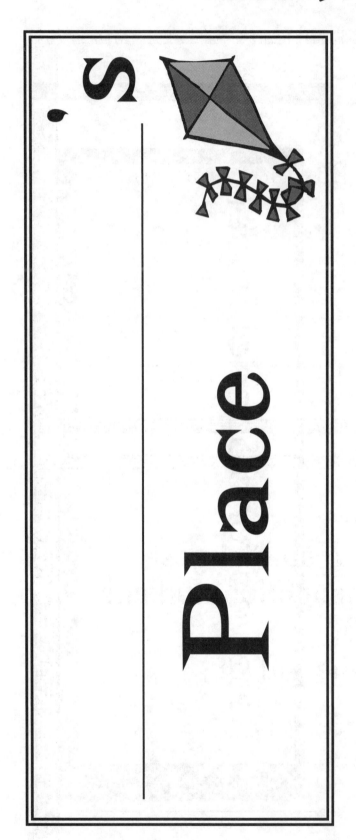

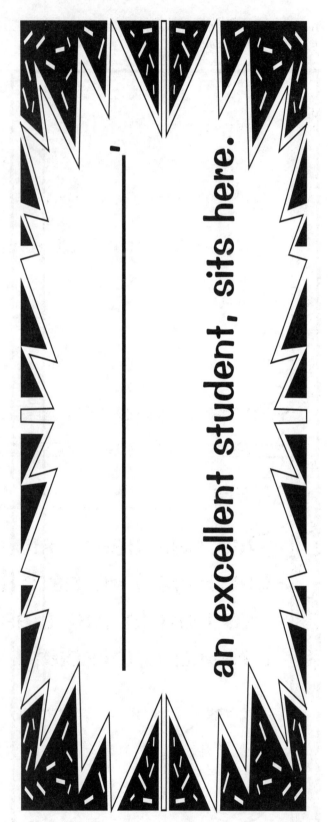

Thank You for the Gift

Dear_____,

Thank you for _____.
You were very thoughtful to remember me in such a way.

Enjoy your vacation!

Thank you.

_____
Signature

Dear_____,

This has been such a special year because I've had thoughtful students like you in my class.
I really appreciate the gift of

_____.

Thank you very much.

_____
Signature

Thank You for Gift (cont.)

Dear_____,

I really appreciate the
_____. I'm sure to use
it often, and when I do
I will think of you.

Thank you.

Dear_____,

Thank you for _____ taking the
time to remember me by making
_____. It was very dear of
you to think of me.

Thank you.

_____
Signature

Birthdays

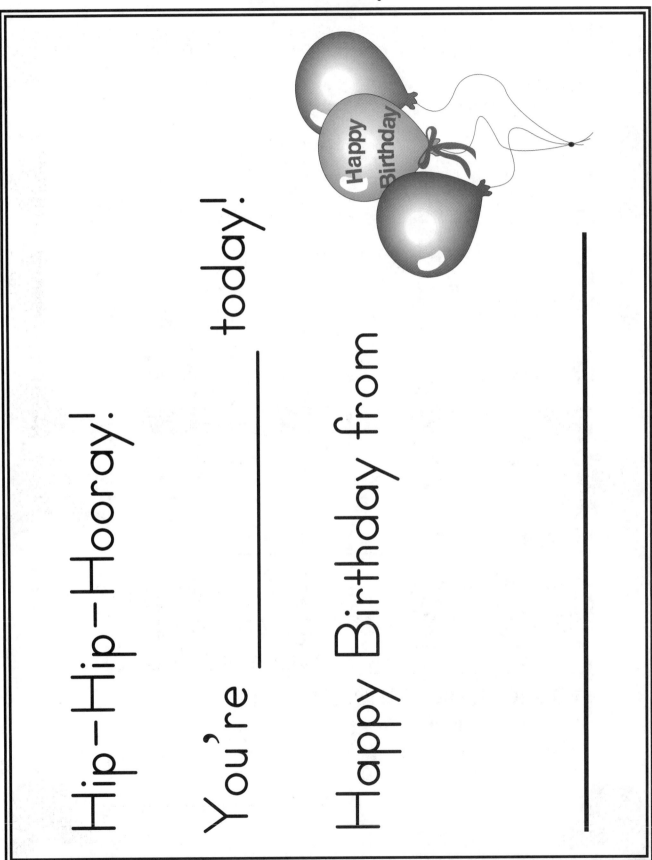

Hip-Hip-Hooray!

You're _____ today!

Happy Birthday from

_____

Birthdays *(cont.)*

Happy birthday to you.

Happy birthday to you.

Happy birthday, dear

Happy birthday to you!

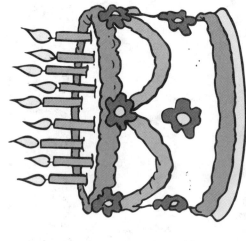

106

Birthdays *(cont.)*

Happy _____ th

Birthday

Birthdays *(cont.)*

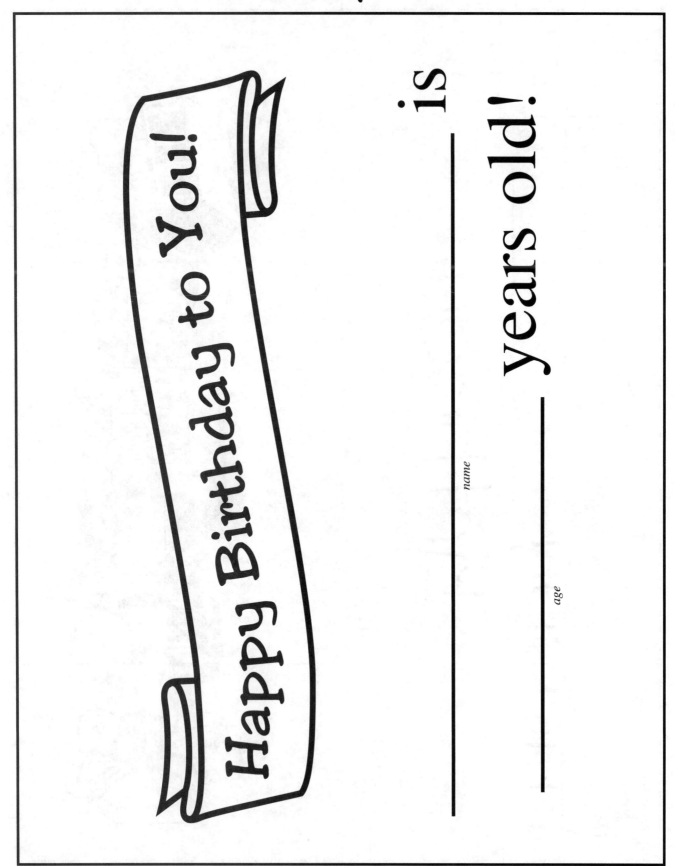

Bookmarks

Teacher Note: *Offer these to students as a reward for good work or behavior.*

The Imagi-Nation

...a great place to visit.

Get Lost in a Good Book

Super Reader

So many books, so little time!

Decorative Borders

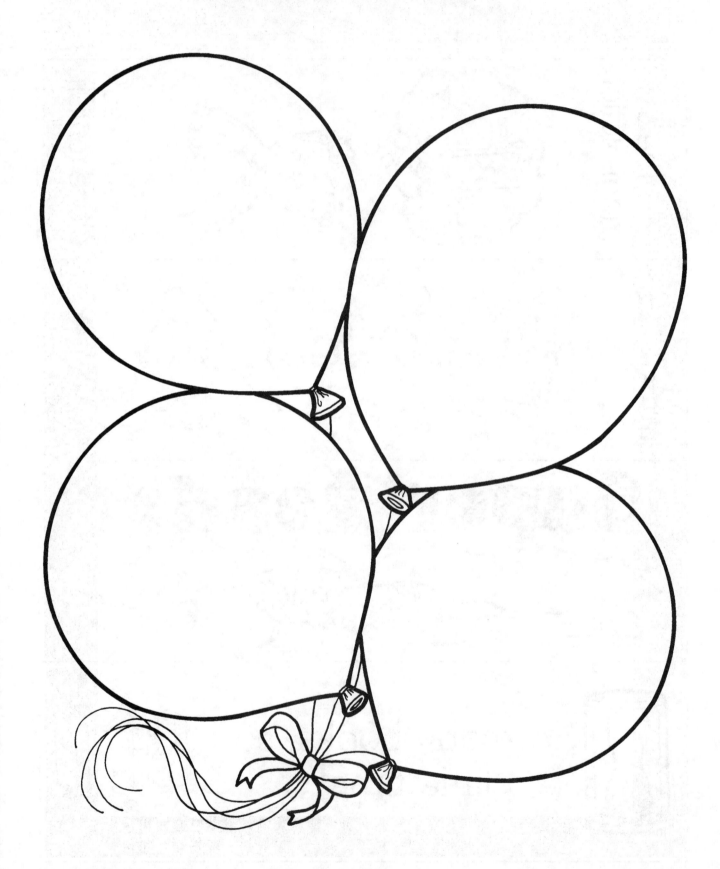

Decorative Borders *(cont.)*

Decorative Borders (cont.)

Decorative Borders (cont.)

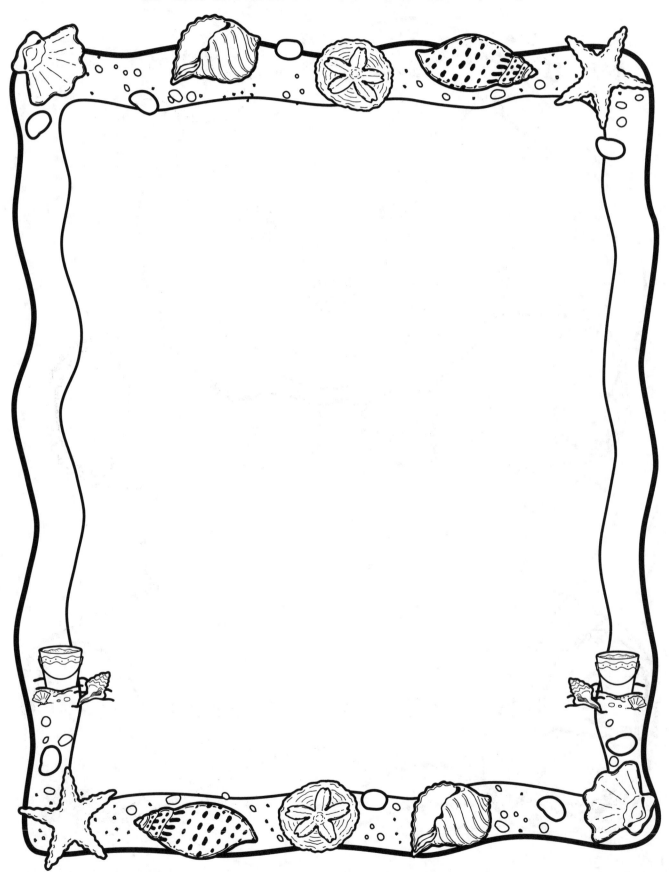

Decorative Borders *(cont.)*

Decorative Borders (cont.)

Decorative Stationery

From the Desk of

Decorative Stationery *(cont.)*

Decorative Stationery *(cont.)*

A Special Reminder

Decorative Stationery *(cont.)*

JANUARY

	SUNDAY	MONDAY	TUESDAY

WEDNESDAY	THURSDAY	FRIDAY	SATURDAY

	SUNDAY	MONDAY	TUESDAY

FEBRUARY

WEDNESDAY	THURSDAY	FRIDAY	SATURDAY

	SUNDAY	MONDAY	TUESDAY

MARCH

WEDNESDAY	THURSDAY	FRIDAY	SATURDAY

	SUNDAY	MONDAY	TUESDAY

APRIL

WEDNESDAY	THURSDAY	FRIDAY	SATURDAY

	SUNDAY	MONDAY	TUESDAY

WEDNESDAY	THURSDAY	FRIDAY	SATURDAY

	SUNDAY	MONDAY	TUESDAY

JUNE

WEDNESDAY	THURSDAY	FRIDAY	SATURDAY

	SUNDAY	MONDAY	TUESDAY

JULY

WEDNESDAY	THURSDAY	FRIDAY	SATURDAY

	SUNDAY	MONDAY	TUESDAY
AUGUST			

WEDNESDAY	THURSDAY	FRIDAY	SATURDAY

SEPTEMBER

SUNDAY	MONDAY	TUESDAY

WEDNESDAY	THURSDAY	FRIDAY	SATURDAY

OCTOBER

	SUNDAY	MONDAY	TUESDAY

WEDNESDAY	THURSDAY	FRIDAY	SATURDAY

NOVEMBER

	SUNDAY	MONDAY	TUESDAY

WEDNESDAY	THURSDAY	FRIDAY	SATURDAY

DECEMBER

	SUNDAY	MONDAY	TUESDAY

142

WEDNESDAY	THURSDAY	FRIDAY	SATURDAY

Notes